Making
MAPLE SYRUP

by Michèle Dufresne

Pioneer Valley Educational Press, Inc.

Here is a maple tree.
Maple **syrup** comes from
maple trees.

Spring is coming.
It is time
to **tap** the trees.

4

There is **sap** in the trees.
The sap will soon
be made into maple syrup.

Make a hole in the tree
with a **drill**.

Hammer the tap into the hole.

Sap from the tree
fills up the bucket.

Cook the sap.
The water will boil away.
Soon the maple syrup
will be thick and sweet!

13

Here are some pancakes
with maple syrup.
Maple syrup is good to eat
on pancakes!

GLOSSARY

drill: a tool with a sharp, pointed end for making holes

sap: the juice of a plant

syrup: thick, sweet boiled liquid

tap: 1. to hit lightly
     2. a tool for getting sap from a tree